BROADWAY CLASSICS

10 of the Best-Loved Songs from Broadway Musicals
Arranged for Late Intermediate to Early Advanced Pianists

Sharon Aaronson

The music in *Top 10 Broadway Classics* originates from some of the world's most outstanding Broadway musicals of the 20th century. This collection contains classic songs of Cole Porter (*Begin the Beguine*), George and Ira Gershwin (*Someone to Watch Over Me*), and Alan Jay Lerner and Frederick Loewe (*Camelot* and *On the Street Where You Live*) as well as the more contemporary classics of Stephen Sondheim (*Send In the Clowns*), Elton John and Tim Rice (*Can You Feel the Love Tonight*) and Alan Menkin and Howard Ashman (*Beauty and the Beast*). Additionally, performers will visit the Land of Oz (*Home* by Charlie Smalls) the gritty era of 1920s Chicago (*And All That Jazz* by Fred Ebb and John Kander), and the bygone worlds of Vaudeville and Burlesque (*Everything's Coming Up Roses* by Stephen Sondheim and Jule Styne).

I was thrilled to have the opportunity to work with this wonderful music. I hope that you find as much pleasure performing these pieces as I did in arranging them for you.

Sharon Aaronson

And All That Jazz (from *Chicago*) (Ebb/Kander) 2

Beauty and the Beast (from Walt Disney's *Beauty and the Beast*) (Menken/Ashman) 27

Begin the Beguine (from *Jubilee*) (Porter) 24

Camelot (from *Camelot*) (Lerner/Loewe) 10

Can You Feel the Love Tonight (from Walt Disney's *The Lion King*) (John/Rice) 34

Everything's Coming Up Roses (from *Gypsy*) (Sondheim/Styne) 6

Home (from *The Wiz*) (Smalls) 21

On the Street Where You Live (from *My Fair Lady*) (Lerner/Loewe) 18

Send In the Clowns (from *A Little Night Music*) (Sondheim) 30

Someone to Watch Over Me (from *Oh, Kay!*) (Gershwin/Gershwin) 14

to Fay, Gerry, Lil, Zelma and Marty, with love

And All That Jazz

(from *Chicago*)

Lyrics by Fred Ebb
Music by John Kander
Arr. by Sharon Aaronson

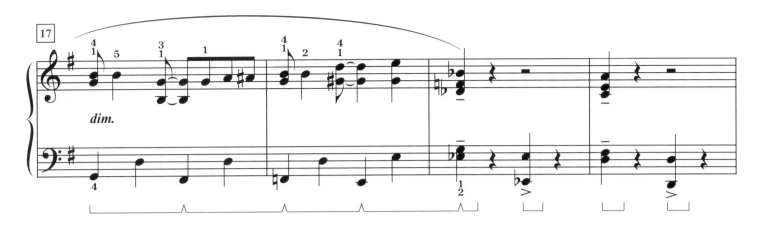

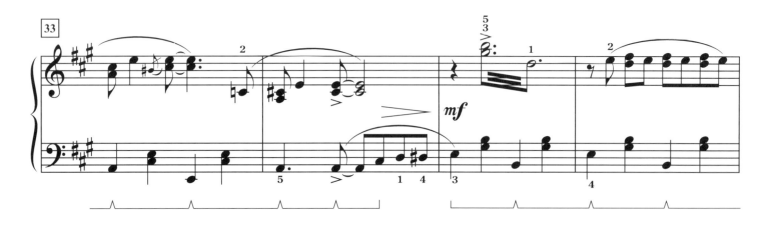

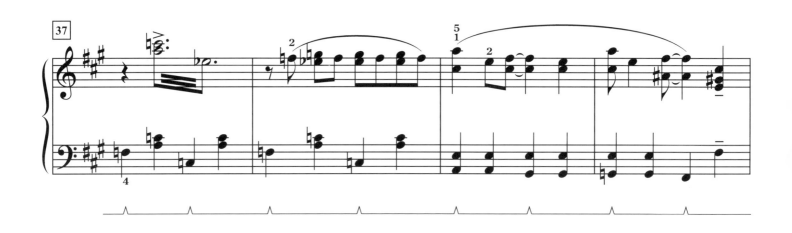

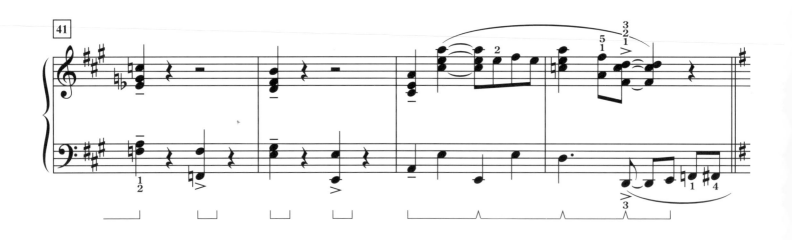

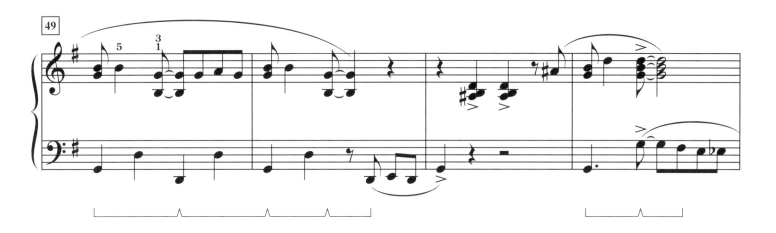

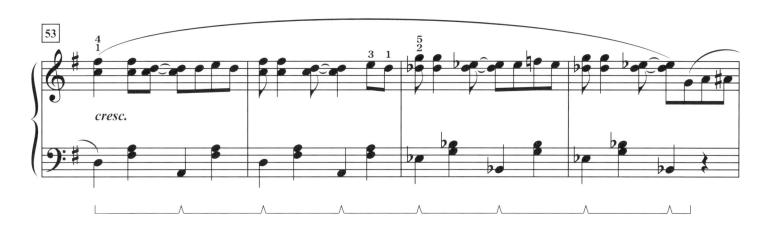

6

Everything's Coming Up Roses

(from *Gypsy*)

Lyrics by Stephen Sondheim
Music by Jule Styne
Arr. by Sharon Aaronson

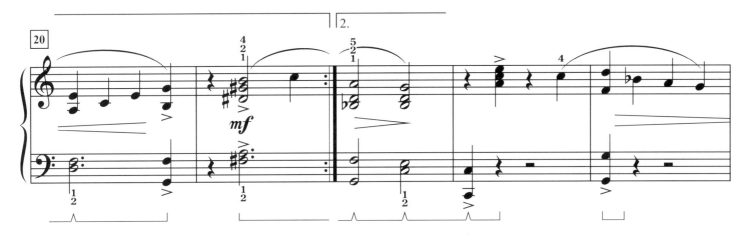

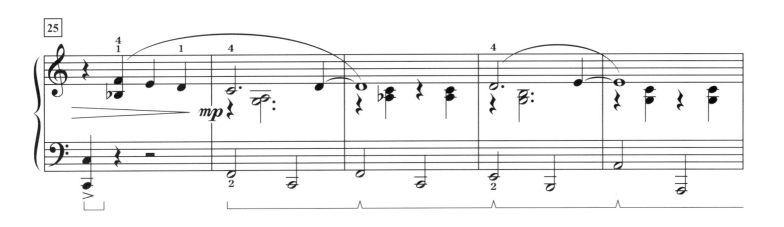

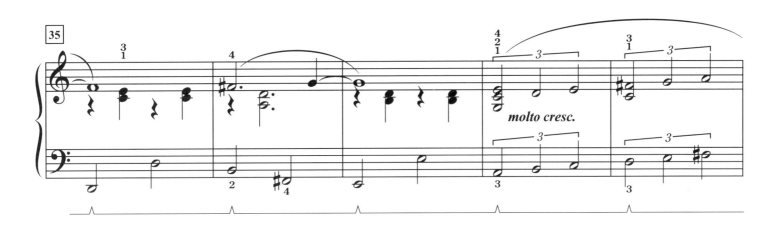

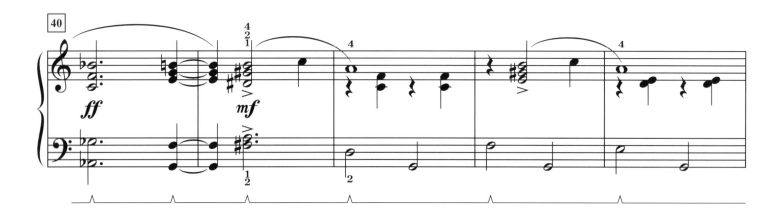

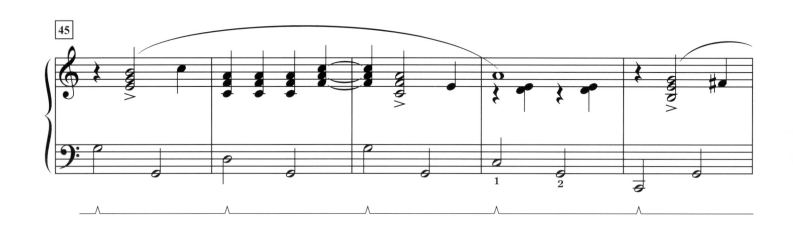

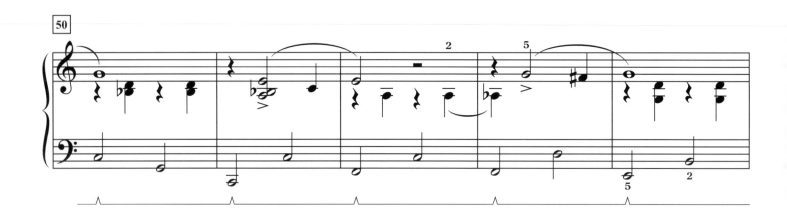

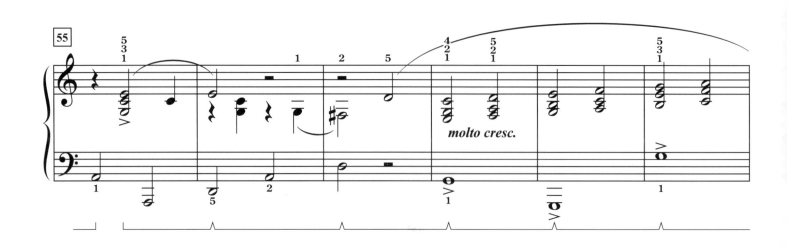

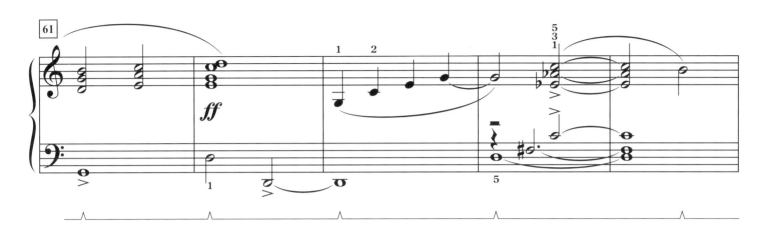

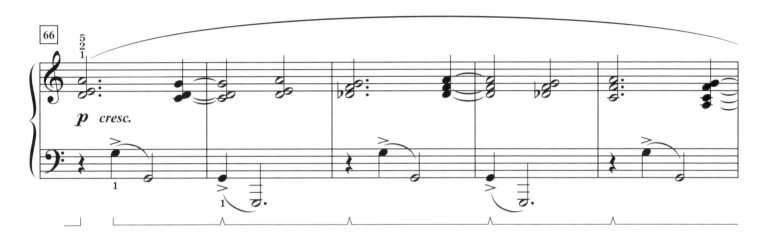

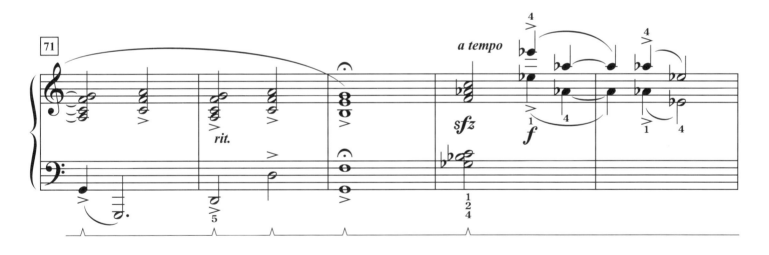

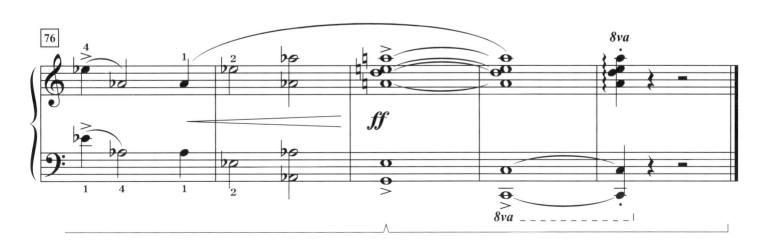

Camelot

(from *Camelot*)

Words by Alan Jay Lerner
Music by Frederick Loewe
Arr. by Sharon Aaronson

12

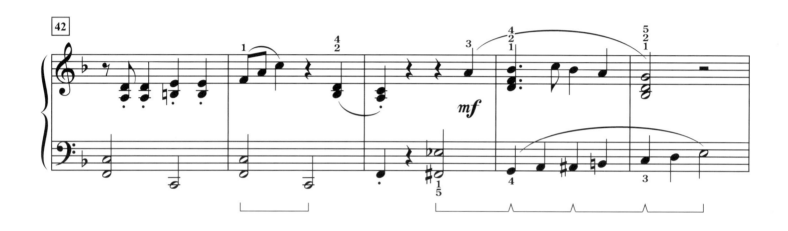

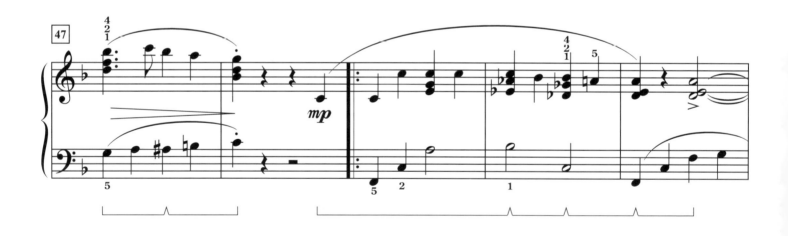

Someone to Watch Over Me

(from *Oh, Kay!*)

Music and Lyrics by George Gershwin and Ira Gershwin
Arr. by Sharon Aaronson

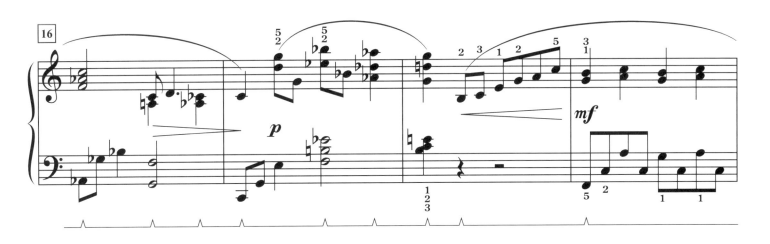

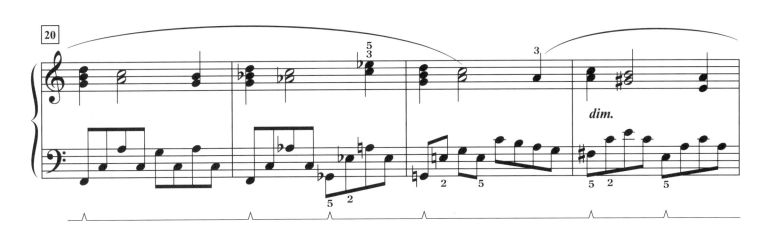

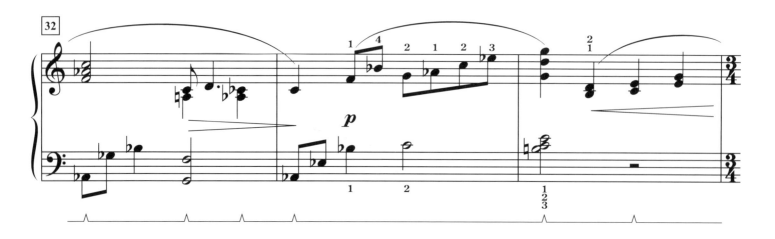

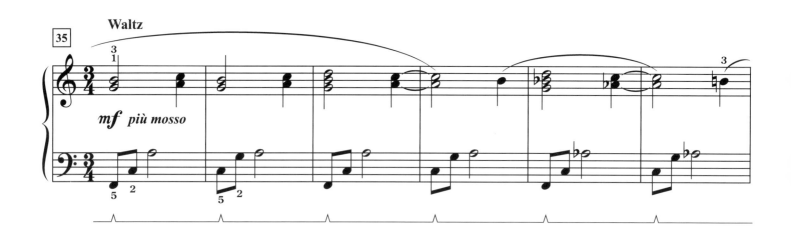

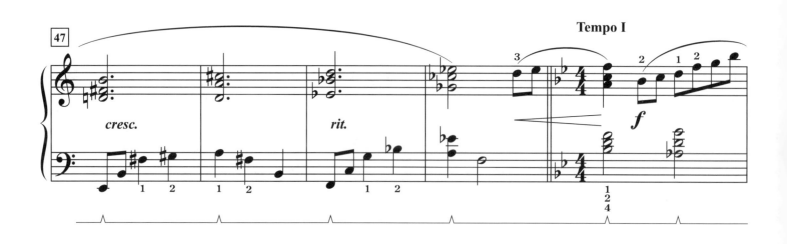

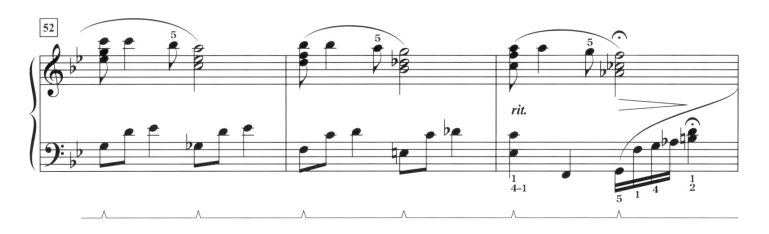

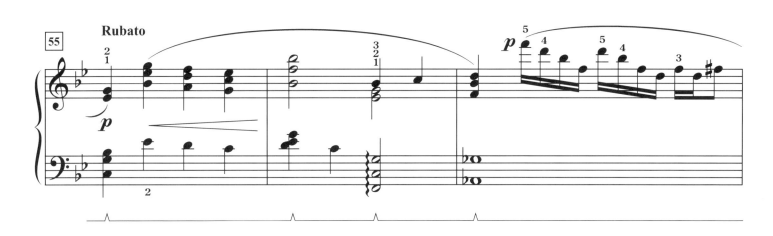

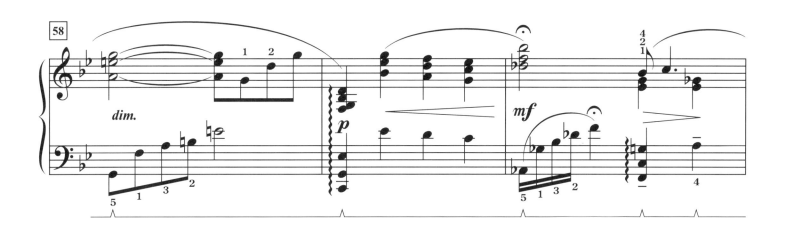

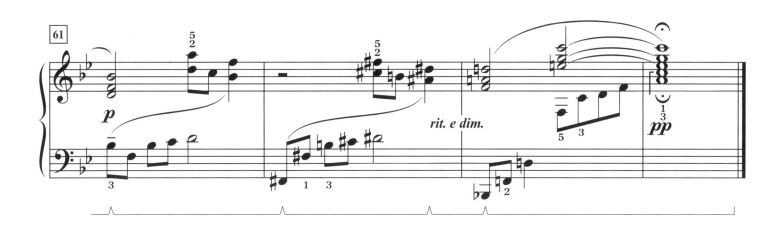

On the Street Where You Live

(from *My Fair Lady*)

Words by Alan Jay Lerner
Music by Frederick Loewe
Arr. by Sharon Aaronson

Home

(from *The Wiz*)

Words and Music by Charlie Smalls
Arr. by Sharon Aaronson

Begin the Beguine

(from *Jubilee*)

Words and Music by Cole Porter

Arr. by Sharon Aaronson

Clementine

It will now be necessary to remember the "flat" throughout the song.

In a cav-ern in a can-yon, ex-ca-va-ting for a mine Lived a
min-er, for-ty nin-er, and his daugh-ter Clem-en-tine. ___ Oh my
dar-ling, oh, my fdar-ling, oh, my dar-ling Clem-en-tine. You are
gone and lost for-ev-er, dread-ful sor-ry, Clem-en-tine. ___

* The thumbs strike the same note. This is permissable.

SUPPLEMENTARY SONG

Silent Night

Si- - - lent Night, Ho- - ly Night. All is calm-
all is bright. 'Round yon vir- - gin Mo-ther and Child,
Ho- ly In- fant so ten-der and mild, Sleep in Hea-ven-ly
Peace. ___ Sleep- - in Hea-ven-ly Peace.

If you desire to play Christmas Carols by the Popular Piano Method, get the book CHRISTMAS SONGS AND CAROLS for Chord Organ- Available from Empire Music Publishers, 934-12th Street, New Westminster, B.C. Canada.

LEFT HAND STUDIES

NEW CHORDS TO MEMORIZE

If further progress is to be made, it is necessary to learn some new chords. Memorize the following chords before continuing.

D MAJOR CHORD

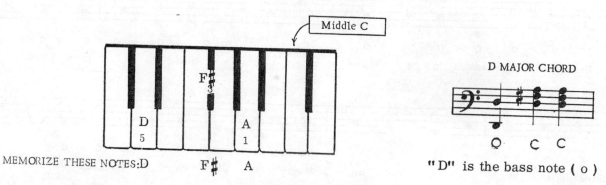

MEMORIZE THESE NOTES: D   F#   A   "D" is the bass note (o)

A MAJOR CHORD

The "A" chord can be sounded in two positions on the keyboard. The position indicated below is the best position at this time, but where the hands cross or interfere with each other, the chord may be sounded one octave lower.

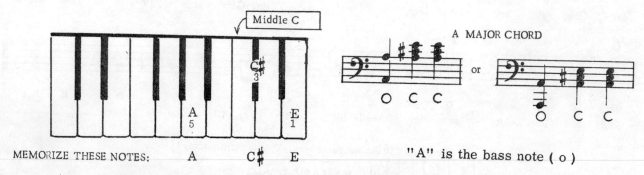

MEMORIZE THESE NOTES: A   C#   E   "A" is the bass note (o)

In The Good Old Summer Time

Shields-Evans

TEACHER NOTE:

(Other inversions of the chords are taught later when student has memorized the definite way of obtaining any chord from the root position.)

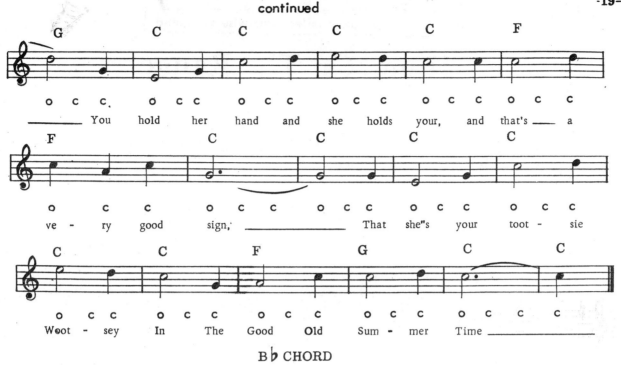

You hold her hand and she holds your, and that's ___ a
ve - ry good sign, _____ That she"s your toot - sie
Woot - sey In The Good Old Sum - mer Time _____

B♭ CHORD

The B♭ chord can be sounded in two locations on the piano keyboard. The position below is the best position at this time, but where the hands cross or interfere with each other, the chord may be sounded one octave lower.

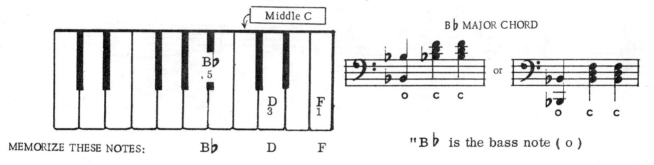

MEMORIZE THESE NOTES: B♭ D F

B♭ MAJOR CHORD

"B♭ is the bass note (o)

Drink Tonight

Donn Dean

Drink To - night and hap - py be, ___ To-
mor - row seems an e - tern - i - ty. ___ But
when you wake up in the morn, ___ You
wish that you'd ne - ver been born. ___

This song uses the C, G, D, and A Major Chords

All "F" notes are sharp unless otherwise indicated.

Home On The Range

Sharp

Oh, give me a home where the buf - fa - lo roam, Where the deer and the

an - te - lope play. _____ Where sel - dom is heard a dis - cou - rag - ing

word, and the skies are not cloud - y all day. _____

Home, _____ home on the range. _____ Where the deer and the

an - te - lope play. _____ Where sel - dom is heard a dis - cou - rag - ing

word, and the skies are not cloud - y all day. _____

* The thumbs strike the same note. This is permissable.

Beauty and the Beast

(from Walt Disney's *Beauty and the Beast*)

Music by Alan Menken
Lyrics by Howard Ashman
Arr. by Sharon Aaronson

Moderately slow

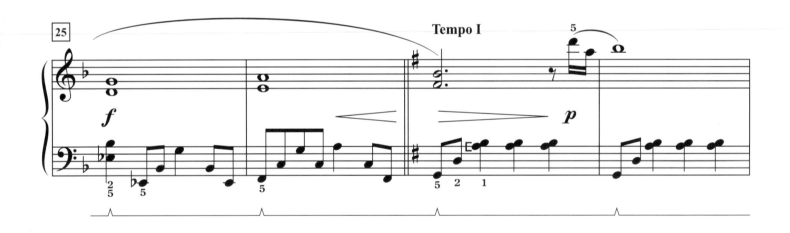

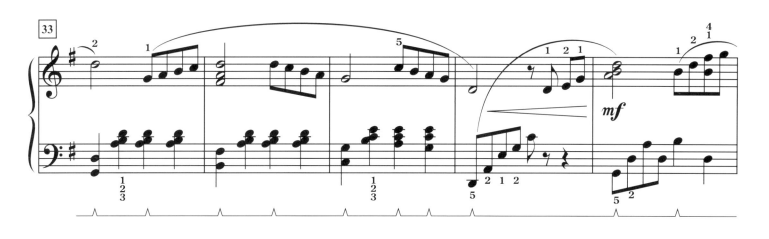

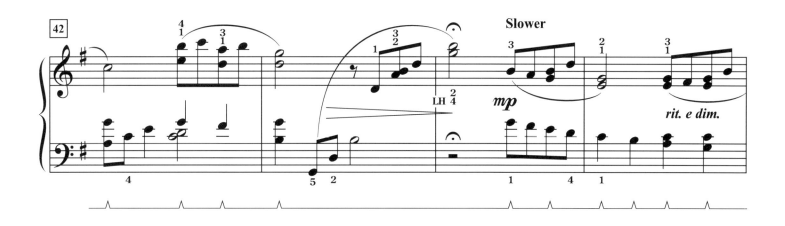
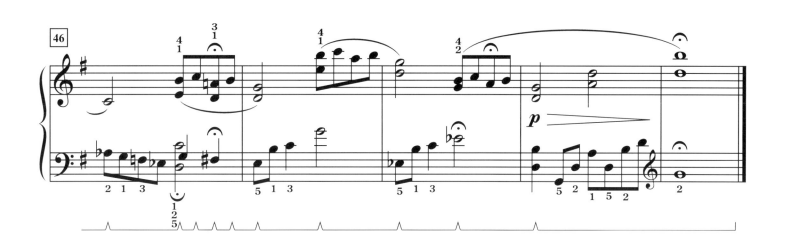

Send In the Clowns

(from *A Little Night Music*)

Music and Lyrics by Stephen Sondheim

Arr. by Sharon Aaronson

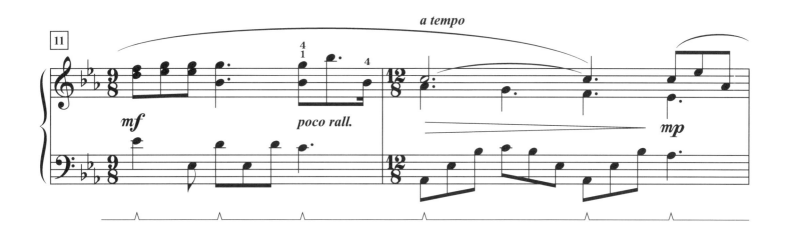

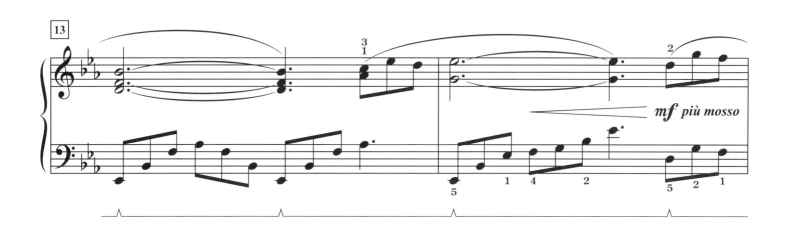

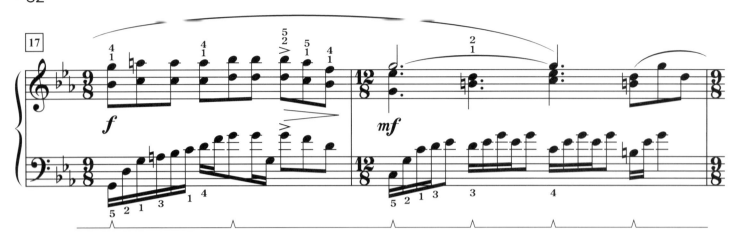

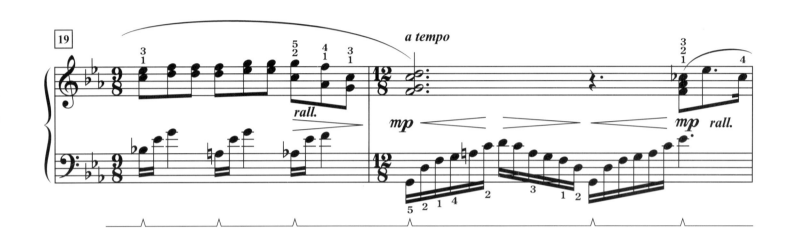

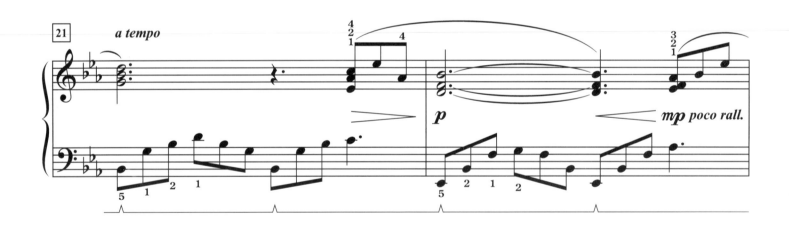

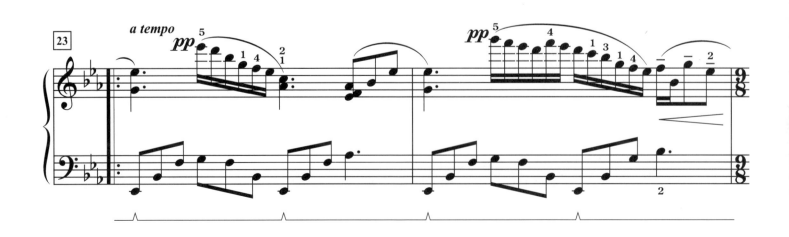

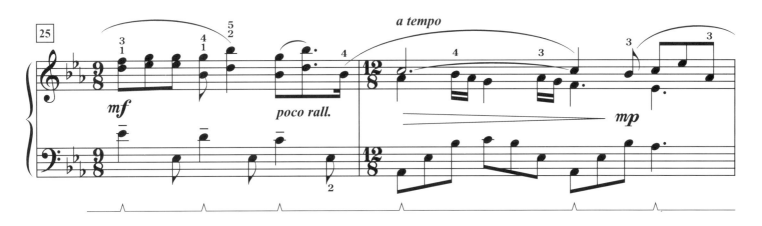

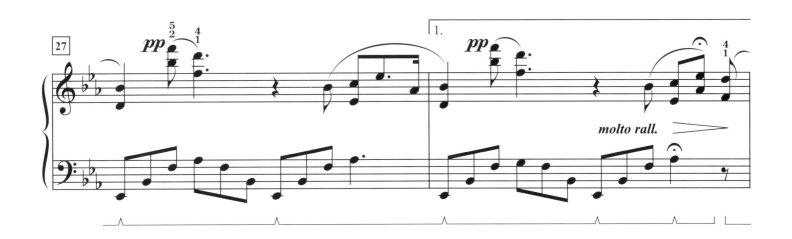

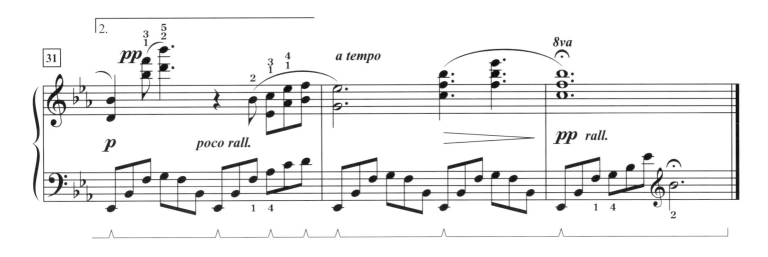

Can You Feel the Love Tonight

(from Walt Disney's *The Lion King*)

Music by Elton John
Words by Tim Rice
Arr. by Sharon Aaronson

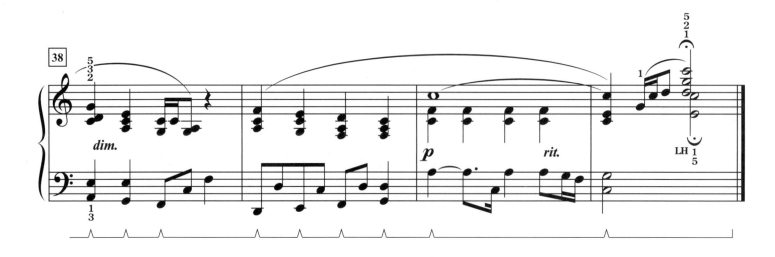